MW01052342

J
796.22
WIL

## DATE DUE

| | | |
|---|---|---|
| JUL 3 1 2004 | | |
| | | |
| SEP 2 9 2004 | | |
| FEB 2 3 2006 | | |
| MAY 1 4 2008 | | |
| | | |
| | | |
| | | |
| | | |
| | | |
| | | |
| | | |
| | | |
| | | |
| | | |

Demco, Inc. 38-293

Rad Sports

# Skateboarding
## Techniques and Tricks

Edward Willett

the rosen publishing group's
rosen
central

BRENTWOOD PUBLIC LIBRARY
8765 Eulalie Ave.
Brentwood, MO  63144

Published in 2003 by The Rosen Publishing Group, Inc.
29 East 21st Street, New York, NY 10010

Copyright © 2003 by The Rosen Publishing Group, Inc.

First Edition

All rights reserved. No part of this book may be reproduced in any form without permission in writing from the publisher, except by a reviewer

**Library of Congress Cataloging-in-Publication Data**

Willett, Edward, 1959–
Skateboarding: Techniques and Tricks / by Edward Willett.— 1st ed.
    p. cm. — (Rad sports)
Includes bibliographical references (p.   ) and index.
ISBN 0-8239-3848-4 (lib. bdg.)
1. Skateboarding—Juvenile literature. [1. Skateboarding.]  I. Title.
II. Series.
GV859.8 .W56 2003
796.22—dc21

                                                          2002005125

*Manufactured in the United States of America*

# CONTENTS

**M**aybe you've seen them on TV. They zip up ramps or halfpipes and leap impossible distances. They turn and flip and somehow come down in one piece. Maybe you've seen them in a city park, hopping over benches, scooting along railings. Maybe you've seen them shoot by you as you trudge your way to school, taking half as much time as you do and having twice as much fun in the bargain.

They're skateboarders, taking part in one of the most challenging, fun, and fastest-growing sports around. And now you're tired of watching them, and you want to try it yourself.

Well, guess what? There's nothing stopping you. It's easy to start skateboarding—but be warned, it's hard to stop! You're likely to find yourself eating and sleeping skateboarding before you're done. Because no matter how good a skateboarder you become, you can always get better with practice. You are limited as to what you can do on a skateboard only by your imagination.

This book will tell you how to choose a skateboard and how to get started using it. It will even provide step-by-step instructions on how to do some basic—and some not-so-basic—tricks.

Stoked? Let's roll!

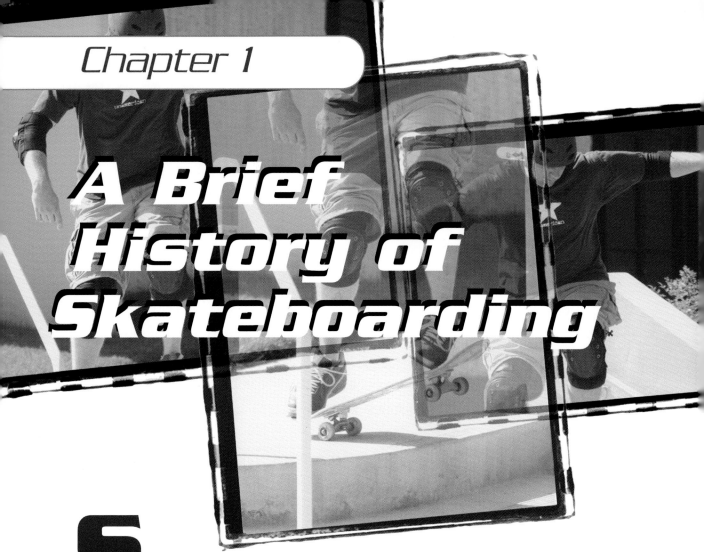

# Chapter 1

# A Brief History of Skateboarding

**S**kateboarding may seem like the ultimate in twenty-first-century coolness, but it's been around a long time. In fact, way back in the 1930s and 1940s, kids used to attach roller skate wheels to the bottoms of two-by-fours to make primitive skateboards.

The first modern skateboard (although still primitive by today's standards) was built and sold at the Val Surf shop in California in 1958. Surfers wanted to surf even when the waves weren't up. They decided to mount skate wheels on square wooden boards.

Skateboarding promptly caught on big time in California, where they called it sidewalk surfing. Competitive skateboarding soon followed. By 1965, the National Skateboard Championships were being covered by ABC's *Wide World of Sports*, and *Life* magazine did a feature on the sport.

The first wave of popularity faded by the end of the 1960s for a couple of reasons. First, the boards really were low tech—and sometimes dangerous. The wheels were made of clay, which meant not only that they were very hard, but that they'd stop turning when they hit a pebble or crack. This would stop the board, but not the skateboarder, who would fly off. You couldn't make tight turns on a 1960s skateboard, either, because the clay wheels didn't have traction.

There were also concerns about safety. Doctors started seeing a lot of kids with skateboarding injuries. Drivers worried about hitting skateboarders. Pedestrians worried about being hit by skateboarders. Some places even passed laws banning skateboarding. And the surfing fad, which had helped to get skateboarding started, faded away.

But there were still some people skateboarding, and they kept trying to improve their boards. In the 1970s, two big improvements helped to revive interest in skateboarding. The most important was the bright idea of Frank Nasworthy. He replaced the clay wheels on his skateboard with urethane wheels. Urethane, a kind of plastic, provided much better traction. It also made for a smoother ride, and it let the wheels on skateboards roll faster.

The 1960s gave us the first skateboard craze. Notice the fat wheels on these early boards.

7

## Skateboarding Hits Pop Culture!

Skateboarding was so popular in the 1960s there was even a song written about it. Jan and Dean, who usually sang songs about surfing, had a minor hit with "Sidewalk Surfing." It uses the same tune as the Beach Boys' "Catch A Wave," and includes the sounds of a skateboard they'd recorded in their driveway. Skateboarding even went to the movies. In 1966, a short film called *Skaterdater* featured skateboarders performing outrageous stunts. It was nominated for an Academy Award!

Skateboarding suddenly became much more exciting. The skateboarders who were still riding began trying much more difficult tricks. They rolled down steeper, winding roads. They skated in cement drainage ditches. They even took their skateboards into empty swimming pools. A lot of people saw how much fun the skateboarders were having. Former skateboarders returned to the sport while new skateboarders took it up daily. All the new interest led manufacturers to make better skateboards than ever before, using parts designed specifically for skateboards, instead of recycling parts designed for roller skates. Better skateboards meant even more exciting tricks could be performed, and that brought even more people into skateboarding.

One major change in skateboards that the new interest in the sport led to was the addition of an upward curve at the back of the board. This kicktail made the board more maneuverable. Many of the tricks skate-boarders perform today would be impossible without it.

The 1970s boom in skateboarding faded, too. Skateboard parks began to close. But oddly enough, that might have been the best thing that could have happened to skateboarding. When the parks closed, skateboarding moved back onto the street—and skateboarders discovered that a whole city was a skatepark. Any ramp or set of steps—or railing—could be a launching pad for tricks.

A new age of skateboarding is now upon America—and the world. Since the X Games competition began in 1995, television has brought millions of kids and teens into the skateboard world. They have responded well. Today, you see skateboarders on the street, skateboarders in skateparks, even skateboarders competing against one another on television to perform the most outrageous stunts. It looks like the boom-and-bust pattern skateboarding followed in its early years is long gone. Skateboards—and skateboarders—are here to stay!

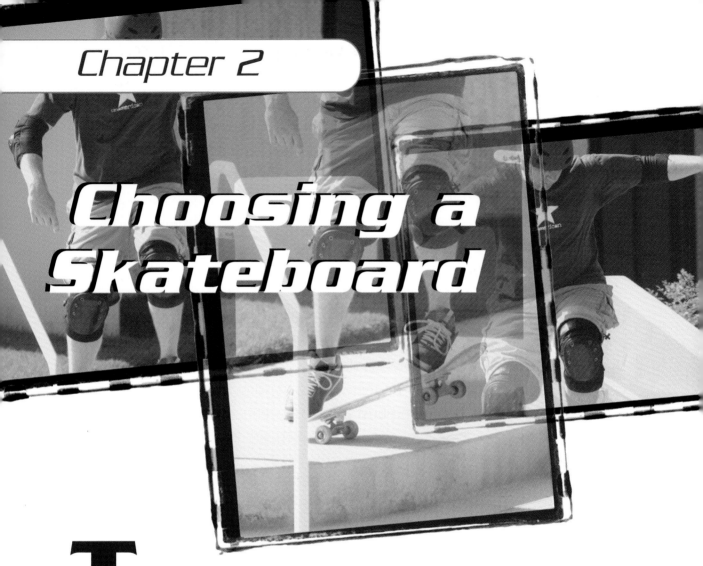

# Chapter 2

# Choosing a Skateboard

There are a lot of different skateboards from which to choose. How do you pick the one that will work best for you? Before you start, you should probably know something about how skateboards are made. Skateboards have three main parts: the deck, the trucks, and the wheels. Looking at each part in more detail will help you to understand how skaters make their boards do what they do.

## The Deck

The deck, board, plank, blank—they all mean the same thing—of a skateboard can be made of many things. Over the years, manufacturers have experimented with boards made from solid planks of wood, fiberglass, aluminum, and molded plastic. Experience and trial and error showed, however, that the best thing out of which to make a skateboard deck is laminated (glued) hardwood plywood. Today, almost all boards are made of

seven layers of Canadian hard rock maple, all glued together. This is better than making a board out of a solid plank of wood, because the board is both strong and flexible. A board made of solid wood, like most boards in the 1960s, is very stiff and can crack or break easily. Flexibility is important because boards have to be able to absorb the impact from a jump or a drop.

Different boards have slightly different shapes, but most boards are curved up at the tail. Some are also turned up at the nose and at the sides. These concave curves make it easier for the skateboarder to move the board with his or her feet.

Most boards come with grip tape attached to the deck's top. Grip tape increases traction. Traction helps skaters move the board and hit tricks. If you buy a board without grip tape, buy some at the skate shop. You will need it.

Today's skateboards are made for durability and come in different sizes. The bottom photo shows a longboard, used for flexibility and cruising.

## Deck Size

Boards come in different sizes. The basic street board is 7 1/2 to 7 3/4 inches wide, and 29 inches long. Shorter boards, say 27 inches, are good for more experienced riders who want to do lots of stunts. Boards designed for vert (riding on ramps) are often wider, maybe 9 inches, and longer, around 30 inches. Boards designed for downhill speed racing are often narrower and longer than the average board.

## Trucks

Skateboard trucks are the steering devices on the bottom of the board to which the wheels are attached. Trucks consist of a metal plate mounted to the base of the board, an axle that pivots on two cushions made of urethane

Skateboard trucks are made of metal for durability. Different kinds of trucks will give skaters tighter or wider turns.

## Self-Expression

Many boards come with fancy graphics on the underside of the board—wild designs and multicolored paint jobs, or lots of decals.

However, many skateboarders prefer to buy a blank board so they can put their own graphics on it. If you're artistic, you can paint your board, or you can just plaster it with decals. Just remember that once you learn how to slide and grind, the underside of the board is going to take a lot of scraping!

(called bushings), and a pivot point. The axles swing on the trucks' pivot points, which allows the skateboard to turn. Lean left, and the left-side axle and wheels pivot toward each other while the right-side axle and wheels pivot away from each other. That makes the skateboard turn left. Lean right, and the skateboard turns right.

Trucks take a lot of punishment. Every time the skateboard turns, they're under stress. Every time the skateboarder does an ollie (a basic jump—more on ollies later) and lands on the board, the trucks have to absorb the shock. So having good trucks on your skateboard is very important.

The best trucks are made of heat-treated aluminum. They have steel axles and steel kingpins (the post that connects the axle to the base plate, which in turn is bolted to the board). The bushings should be nice and springy to ensure a smooth ride.

## Wheels

Like everything else on skateboards, wheels come in many different sizes and styles. Street skaters prefer smaller wheels because they help the board roll

Skateboard wheels are measured according to hardness. Most bearings come enclosed to keep out dirt.

faster. Ramp skaters like larger wheels because they provide more control. Downhill skaters like even larger wheels. Wheel sizes are measured in millimeters (mm). Most skateboarders use wheels between 50 and 60 mm in diameter.

The other choice when it comes to wheels is their hardness. Wheel hardness, or the wheel's durometer, is measured on a scale of 1 to 100, with 1 being about as soft as a rubber eraser accidentally left on a hot stove top, and 100 being about as hard as your average rock.

Most skateboards today have wheels with a durometer somewhere in the 90s. Again, what the skateboard is going to be used for influences the choice of wheel. Ramp skaters like a harder wheel because it gives them more speed and breaks loose of the surface more easily—very important when your goal is to leap into the air at the top of the ramp! Street skaters like a slightly softer wheel to give a smoother ride on rough surfaces while still breaking loose of the surface easily enough to enable them to do tricks. Downhill skaters usually like a softer wheel for more traction through tight turns.

## Wheel Bearings

One of the biggest improvements in skateboards came in the 1970s with the introduction of sealed bearings. Before that, bearings were open to

## Roller Skates in a Ballroom?

Although today's trucks are made specifically for skate-boards, they're based on a design that's more than seventy years old. In the 1920s, there was a big fad for ballroom dancing on roller skates. The "Chicago pivot" was invented to give ballroom roller skaters more control. When the first modern skateboards were built, the Chicago pivot was used on them, too.

The 1920s design has been refined over the years to allow better turning and improve stability—but it's still recognizable as the Chicago pivot.

the air—and any grit that happened to be flying around. They didn't last long and they were very noisy. Today's sealed bearings last longer and make the boards quieter.

## So Many Choices

With so many choices, how do you know which skateboard is right for you? The best advice is to talk to the sales staff at a good skateboard shop. They can recommend boards that fit your size, your long-term skateboarding plans, and your budget. After all, you're just getting started—you won't be riding ramps or even doing ollies for a while. On the other hand, you want a board that will last.

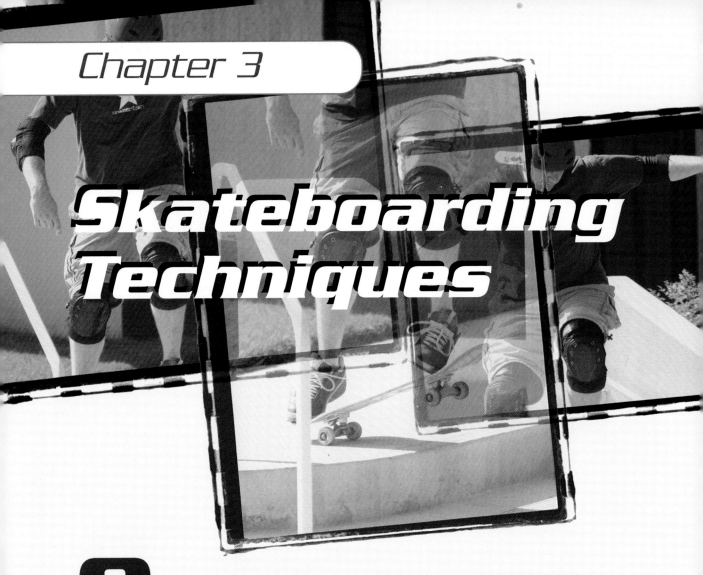

# Chapter 3

# Skateboarding Techniques

**O**K, you have your skateboard, you have your safety gear (see Chapter 5), and you have your cool skateboarding clothes. It looks like you're ready to do some serious thrashin'. Yet there's another question to be answered: If you've never skated before, what do you do next?

If you've tried standing on your board, you already know "serious thrashin'" isn't something you're going to be doing any time soon. Just standing still may seem to be enough of a challenge.

Don't worry. Remember the first time you tried to ride a bicycle? Learning to skateboard is a lot like learning to cycle. It takes a good sense of balance and a lot of practice.

## Standing

Hold onto something while you stand on your board. By standing on the board you'll get a better idea of how your feet fit on it, how wobbly it is, and how much it tips forward and backward.

Bend your knees slightly and shift your weight forward to your toes, then back toward your heels to make the board wobble from side to side. Shift your weight from one foot to the other to tip it forward and backward.

One thing you may be able to figure out while you're standing still is whether you have a regular stance or are a goofy-foot. "Goofy-foot" isn't an insult; it just means that you like to stand with your right foot forward (like Tony Hawk). A left-foot forward stance is called regular foot (the way Andy Macdonald rides). Try standing on the board both ways and use the stance that feels most comfortable.

The first step to learning how to skateboard is balancing on the board. If you can stand without losing your balance, you're ready to glide.

## Gliding

Once you've got a feel for the board while standing still, it's time to try gliding. Find a flat, smooth surface—an empty parking lot, a skatepark, or a long driveway.

If you're not sure yet if you have a regular stance or a goofy-foot stance, this is the time to find out. Try gliding a few times, using first one foot on the front of the board, then the other. You're sure to find one way or the other more comfortable. Try gliding one-footed at first. When you feel comfortable with your balance (and stance), it's time to glide two-footed.

## One-Foot Gliding

**1.** Put one foot on the board, behind the front wheels, pointed straight toward the front. Make sure you leave room for your back foot (you won't be riding with both feet on the board right away, but you should start putting your feet in the proper position now). Don't put your front foot so far forward that the board tips onto its nose.

**2.** Now give a little push with your back foot. This is called pedaling. Glide forward and ride with only your front foot on the board. Don't be alarmed if the board gets away from you a couple of times, or even if you fall once or twice. It's all part of practicing. Before long, you'll start to feel more secure on the board.

# Two-Foot Gliding

**1.** Push off and pedal.

**2.** Stand with two feet on the board. Put your back foot sideways across the board, then turn your front foot so it's across the board, too. Be sure to bend your knees a little, and keep your feet apart—a wide stance gives you more stability.

# Stopping

The two best ways to stop while skateboarding are either bailing or foot dragging. Both are safe ways to stop quickly.

## Bailing

**1.** To bail you need only step off the board (bail) toward the front with a running motion.

## 2 Bailing (continued)

**2.** As you come off the board and onto the ground, use your front foot to kick the board backward slightly. This keeps the board from rolling ahead of you. You should be able to pull yourself to a stop within a few steps.

Once you stop, turn around and use your foot to stop the board. Bailing is that easy.

# The Foot-Drag

**1.** Keep your front foot on the board, over the front wheel for stability. Bring your rear foot off the board and drag it on the ground. Use gentle pressure on the ground at first.

**2.** Increase the pressure on your rear foot drag until you get the amount of braking you want.

You can foot drag to a complete stop, or use your foot to slow down and then bail. Whether going fast or slow, the foot drag is a good braking technique.

# Turning

Skateboarding would be pretty boring if you could only travel in straight lines. The whole idea of surfing the streets is to turn, glide, and do tricks. There are two kinds of basic turns: a frontside turn and a backside turn. A frontside turn is a turn in the direction your toes are pointing. A backside turn is a turn in the direction your heels are pointing.

Turning a skateboard is simply a matter of leaning the board in the direction you want to go. To do a frontside turn, shift your weight to your toes. To do a backside turn, shift your weight to your heels. Try to limit your upper-body movement. Think of your body as being divided into two halves

Balancing on the board during a turn requires knowing your center of gravity. Your center of gravity is the position that your body needs to be in when you move and turn to keep yourself from toppling over. While turning on a skateboard, you need to lean into your turns to hold your center of gravity.

at the waist. Use the lower half of your body to turn the board, while keeping your upper half pointing in the direction you're going. And try not to watch your feet. You need your head up and your eyes facing front so you can see where you're going and avoid running into anything.

Practice your turning on a flat surface. Push off and start gliding, and try a few gentle turns. Do a frontside turn and then a backside turn as you travel forward, drawing a letter S. You'll soon learn just exactly how much pressure you need to apply to get the effect you want. When you're ready, you can sharpen your turns by leaning harder into them.

Keep practicing gliding and turning until riding a skateboard begins to feel like second nature to you. You may get it in a few hours, or it may take much longer. Don't be impatient. Even the best skateboarder you've ever seen started just the way you have. Eventually you'll get the hang of it, and then you can start working on the next step: tricks.

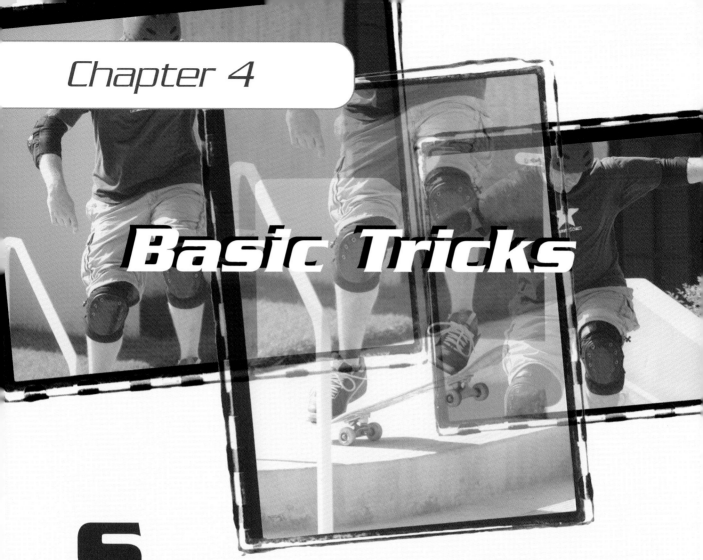

# Chapter 4

# Basic Tricks

**S**kateboarding today is all about doing tricks. But before you can do tricks like a pro, you have to start small. The following tricks are the basic skateboard tricks that all skateboarders must know.

The fact is, skateboarding tricks are generally made up of combinations of other tricks. If you learn some basic moves, you'll find more complicated moves easier to master. You'll also have the skills you need in order to invent some moves of your own.

## Wheelies

A wheelie lets you ride on your back wheels. The trick to doing good wheelies is keeping your balance.

Wheelies

**1.** Push off and glide forward.

**2.** Shift your weight back and lift the front wheels off the ground.

**3.** Keep your front foot over the front wheels and use the tail to help hold your balance.

Practice the wheelie until you can easily lift the front wheels and glide along without tipping back or letting the front wheels fall forward to the ground. You can drag both the board's tail and your heel to scrub off speed.

A different kind of wheelie is the tic-tac. Once you've lifted the board's nose into the air, use your front foot to move the nose either left or right. The trick is to keep the nose in the air as you bring it left and right. Finish the tic-tac by pointing the nose straight ahead and dropping the wheels. If you do the tic-tac correctly, you'll find that it helps to move the board forward.

# Kickturns

The kickturn is a tic-tac taken to the extreme. What you're doing is making a quick turn by first doing a wheelie, then dropping the front wheels to change direction. Kickturns need to be done at slow speeds. There is a 90-degree kickturn, a 180-degree kickturn, and a 360-degree kickturn. The trick to each of these turns is keeping your balance through the turn. You need to watch how your weight shifts as you turn or spin, while keeping up your momentum after the turn.

## 90-Degree Kickturn

**1.** Push off and glide forward at a slow speed. Raise the board to a low wheelie.

**2.** Move the nose of the board left or right quickly and drop it to the ground.

**3.** When the front wheels hit you'll be moving in that direction. Make sure you bend your legs and lean your body into the turn. Otherwise you'll go forward as the board takes its turn.

## 180-Degree Kickturn

A 180-degree kickturn turns you halfway around to point back in the direction from which you came.

**1.** Push off and glide forward slowly. Lift the front wheels.

**2.** Use your legs to whip the board around 180 degrees (facing the opposite direction). Keep your upper body vertical and keep your arms out for balance.

**3.** Drop the front wheels. You should be pointing in the opposite direction now. If you've done the 180 kickturn well, you'll have momentum to move forward after the turn. If not, either tic-tac or pedal to gain speed.

## 360-Degree Kickturn

A 360-degree kickturn is a complete spin that leaves you facing the same way as when you started.

**1.** Push off and lift the front wheel up.

**2.** As you lift the front wheel, use your legs and body to spin yourself in a complete circle (360 degrees).

**3** 360-Degree Kickturn (continued)

**3.** When you come around and are pointing in the same direction as when you started, drop the wheel and push off to gain speed.

# The Drop

Another basic move is the drop. This is just what it sounds like—a drop from a higher level to a lower level. Probably the most common drop is from the

**1.** Push off and roll forward at a moderate speed.

**2.** As you come to the spot that drops off, shift your weight back. Set your back foot against the tail. Lift the front wheels as you go over the edge. Shift your back foot over the axle in the air.

**3.** Flex your knees to push the board down for the landing. Hit with both sets of wheels at the same time and ride away. Try to land with your feet over the trucks for maximum control.

sidewalk to the street. Drops require more than just rolling off the edge of something and landing. That's likely to tip you off headfirst as the nose drops.

## The Ollie

The ollie is probably the most famous of all skateboarding tricks. It's the trick you use to jump over obstacles.

**1.** Lift your back foot and drop it down hard on the tail.

**2.** Lift your front foot as your back foot hits the tail. As the tail strikes the ground, the board bounces up into the air and begins to pitch forward.

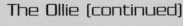

## The Ollie (continued)

**3.** While the board is in the air, slide your front foot forward to drag the board even higher. Then lift the back foot to catch the tail. Your rear foot comes firmly in contact with the board again. Now the board will level out in the air for just a moment.

**4.** Come down over the wheels with your legs bent to absorb the landing. When the wheels hit, you should have enough momentum to roll away.

Learn the ollie while standing still before you do it while rolling. Always start with your feet over the front and back wheels.

The ollie is the basis of all kinds of additional tricks. Variations on the ollie are the nollie (a backwards ollie), the ollie 180 (turning mid-air so you come down facing the other way), and the ollie 360 (doing a complete revolution while in the air). Once you learn to ollie well, a whole world of new tricks will open up to you.

# Backside Boardslide

Because the urban world is full of things to slide on, slides are a basic part of street skating. In a slide, you skid the bottom of the board along a surface edge—a curb or a low wall, for instance—at right angles to the direction you're moving. You need to know how to ollie to do a slide. When you start practicing slides, start with low objects like curbs or low walls. Make sure the curb or wall edge is smooth. Place the bottom of your board over the edge and move it forward. If your board moves easily, you can do a slide easily. If the edge is rough, you're likely to fall while trying to slide on it.

The trick to slides is keeping your shoulders square to the direction in which the board is going.

**1.** To do a backside boardslide, push off and roll forward back-side (your back facing the slide obstacle) toward the low wall at a shallow angle.

**2.** As you come up to the slide obstacle, ollie and rotate the board 90 degrees. Come down on the bottom of the deck with your feet over the wheels for balance. You'll be facing forward as you slide along the edge.

**3**

Backside Boardslide (continued)

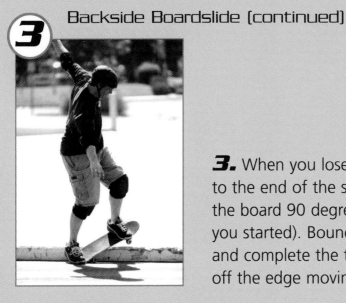

**3.** When you lose speed or come to the end of the slide, start turning the board 90 degrees (back the way you started). Bounce on the board and complete the turn so you come off the edge moving forward.

# 50-50 Grind

Grinds are similar to slides. The difference is that instead of sliding on the bottom of the board, you slide on the metal trucks. You can slide either on the nose truck, the tail truck, or both. The most basic grind is the 50-50.

The trick to grinds is getting the trucks above the grindable surface quickly and setting the trucks onto the grind edge. It's a matter of a good approach and a smooth ollie that will give you the best position to complete all grinds.

**1.** Push off and roll toward the grind edge at a 30-degree angle or less.

**2.** Ollie and bring the trucks above the grinding edge.

**3.** Land on the trucks—not the wheels—with your feet over the wheels. As you grind, your shoulders should be square to the direction you're moving.

**4.** When you slow down or come to the end, bounce on the board and lift it up and off the edge. Land on the wheels and ride away.

# Chapter 5

# Safety and Maintenance

**L**ike all sports, skateboarding can be dangerous. Any time you combine speed, hard surfaces, and the soft human body, there's a possibility of injury. Skateboarding can be made a lot safer if you take some basic precautions.

## Protective Gear

According to the U.S. Consumer Product Safety Commission (CPSC), approximately 26,000 people are treated in hospital emergency rooms each year with skateboard-related injuries. These injuries include sprains, breaks, bruises, and scrapes. Safety gear and practicing safe skating help to prevent injury.

## Helmet

No pro rides without a helmet. Look at Tony Hawk, Andy Macdonald, or Bob Burnquist. The helmet is the most important part of a skater's safety gear. Buy a helmet that fits snugly, but is not too tight. Your helmet should have a chinstrap, too.

Buy a helmet—and all safety gear—that has been approved by the Consumer Product Safety Commission. All products carrying the CPSC safety-approved label have been tested for durability and use.

## Elbow and Knee Pads

Wearing elbow and knee pads will save you many trips to the emergency room. You'll also learn to live with a lot fewer scars from scrapes and cuts. Why? Because when you skate, you will fall.

Elbow and knee pads are made of foam padding covered by nylon cloth. They are fixed onto your elbows and knees with Velcro straps. For added safety,

Skateboard safety begins with wearing a helmet. Elbow and knee pads are important, too. Skateboard riding is done on hard surfaces, and the first time you fall, you'll be glad you're wearing the gear.

buy pads that also have high-impact, hard plastic caps that cover the pads covering your joints.

## Wrist Guards

Wrist guards slip over your hands and fit over your wrists and up to your forearms. They act as cushions to prevent scrapes. They also help stop your wrists from bending backwards when you hold your hands out to take a fall.

# Learning to Fall

No matter how careful you are, you will fall again and again while skating. So do what wrestlers and sky divers and other athletes who do a lot of falling do: practice it. Find a soft surface like grass or a gym mat. Then practice bending your knees and lowering your body as you fall. Roll yourself into a ball (which protects your limbs and head) and let yourself roll over and over.

Wrist guards prevent scrapes, breaks, and twists during falls. Beginners should wear them every time out.

If you stay relaxed and flexible when you fall, you will likely avoid injury. Tightening up, or falling while stiff, is a sure way to hit hard and hurt yourself. Most important, learn not to reach out with your hands to stop yourself as you fall. That's a good way to break your wrists when you take a tumble from a skateboard onto pavement!

# Other Safety Tips

Besides safety gear, riding safely is the best way to avoid injury. These tips are tried and true for skaters of all abilities:

1. Wear proper clothing. High-top sneakers are a good idea; sneakers grip the board better than other kinds of shoes, and high-tops provide more support for your ankles. Long pants will help protect your skin if you fall.
2. Watch out for traffic. Even safety equipment won't help you if you lose an argument with an oncoming car. Never ride in the middle of the street or in heavy traffic, or on a slope that could dump you into traffic if you lose control. And never, ever hitch a ride from a car, bus, truck, motorcycle, or even a bicycle.
3. Stay dry. Don't skate when the pavement is wet. Urethane wheels don't have any treads. When the pavement is wet, they lose grip, which means the board could slip sideways out from under you at the worst possible time.
4. Be patient. Don't try difficult tricks before you're ready. It takes a lot of practice to ride well. Don't try something just because someone else does.

## Board Maintenance

Keeping your board in tip-top shape helps it last and helps prevent injury. Before each riding session, inspect your board for loose, broken, or cracked parts. All skateboard parts wear out, but they don't all wear out at the same rate.

## Repair

You can extend the life of your skateboard by performing some basic repair and tune-up on it yourself. (Major problems should be dealt with by a properly trained repair person, of course.) Skateboard maintenance requires a wrench. You can buy one that has multiple uses and fits in your pocket. Having it with you lets you perform basic maintenance on the fly.

## Wheels

Urethane wheels are soft and are constantly in contact with whatever it is you're skating on. Therefore they tend to wear out first. In fact, if you skateboard on a daily basis, your wheels may only last for a couple of months. You can't keep them from wearing out, but you can rotate them just like tires on a car so they at least wear evenly.

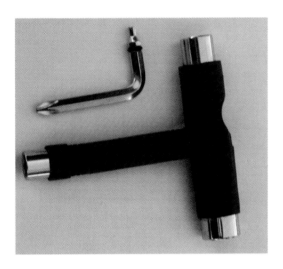

Having a multiuse tool in your pocket will let you fix or adjust your board anywhere you ride.

## Deck Problems

A skateboard's wood deck will eventually crack and splinter. There's no way to prevent this common wear problem. Small cracks shouldn't worry you as much as cracks that break through several layers of your board. Most pros will use their board until it breaks in half. If you feel a big difference in your board's performance because of cracks, it's time to buy a new board.

Keeping your grip tape gripping is important for both your enjoyment and safety. Like sandpaper, grip tape can get clogged with grime and lose its grip. Spray it with household cleaner or warm water and scrub it with a soft-bristle brush to clean it. Grip tape can last as long as your deck if you take care of it.

## Truck Maintenance

The bushings in the truck are made of a soft material and also take a beating. If the bushings are in good shape and are properly adjusted, you should be able to see only three or four threads of the kingpin exposed over the adjustment nut.

Check the self-locking nuts with which the trucks and wheels are mounted, too. If you can spin them with your fingers, they're badly worn and need to be replaced right away.

# Happy Skating!

This book has only scratched the surface of what's waiting for you as a skateboarder. The basic moves and tricks described in the last two chapters will get you started, but how far you go in the sport depends on you. If you really love it, practice hard, keep yourself and your board in top-notch condition, and above all skate safely—you want to be skateboarding for many years to come, right?

You can even skateboard competitively. Most cities have skateboarding exhibitions or competitions. Hang out at these events to learn new tricks and meet other people interested in skateboarding. Find out from the organizers how you can get involved as a volunteer. Eventually, when you think you're ready, enter an event. Keep practicing, and keep competing, and maybe someday you'll be skateboarding at the Olympics. (Skateboarding will be a demonstration sport in the 2004 Summer Olympic Games in Athens, Greece.)

Whether you ever skateboard at the Olympics or ever compete at all doesn't really matter, though. The bottom line is, skateboarding is fun.

So what are you waiting for? You've read the book, now live the life. Get skating!

# Glossary

**air** Riding a board with all four wheels off the ground.

**backside** Any trick or turn performed with the skater's back facing the ramp or obstacle.

**bail** To jump off the board while it's in motion.

**bearings** Small metal balls that help the wheels spin smoothly.

**bushings** Rubbery components that surround the kingpin and aid in turning and cushioning the ride.

**carve** To skate in a long, curving arc.

**deck** The part of a skateboard you stand on, usually made of laminated maple.

**durometer** The hardness of urethane used to make a wheel, measured by a number between 1 and 100.

**frontside** Any trick or turn performed with the front of the skater's body facing the ramp or obstacle.

**goofy-foot** Riding with the right foot forward.

**grind** Scraping one or both trucks on a surface.

**grip tape**  A tape that's sticky on one side and like sandpaper on the other; used to increase friction between the deck and the skater's feet.

**halfpipe**  A U-shaped ramp.

**kingpin**  The bolt that holds the hanger to the baseplate.

**nollie**  A backwards ollie, in which the skater taps the nose of the board instead of the tail.

**nose**  The front of the skateboard, from the front truck to the end.

**ollie**  The basic move on which most skating tricks are based; a jump performed by tapping the tail of the board on the ground.

**regular foot**  Riding with the left foot forward.

**slide**  Sliding the underside of the deck along an object, such as a curb or handrail.

**stance**  The way you stand on your board—regular or goofy.

**street skating**  Skating on streets, curbs, and other urban fixtures, such as railings and benches.

**switch stance**  Riding with the opposite foot forward from which you normally use.

**tail**  The back of the skateboard, from the back truck to the end

**tailslide**  Sliding the underside of the tail end of a board on something.

**tic-tac**  To pivot left and right on your back wheels.

**trucks**  The axle assemblies that connect the wheels to the deck and make it possible to turn the board.

**vert skating**  Skating on ramps and other structures specifically made for skating, in a skatepark, for example.

**wheelbase**  The distance between the front and back wheels.

# For More Information

## Organizations

### IASC (International Association of Skateboard Companies)

Box 37
Santa Barbara, CA 93116
(805) 683-5676
Web site: http://www.skateboardiasc.org

### Skateboarding Association of America

6140 Ulmerton Road
Clearwater, FL 33760
(727) 523-0875
Web site: http://www.skateboardassn.org

## Skatepark Association of the United States of America

2118 Wilshire Boulevard, #622
Santa Monica, CA 90403
(310) 453-7885
Web site: http://www.spausa.org

## USA (United Skateboarding Association)

P.O. Box 986
New Brunswick, NJ 08903
(732) 432-5400 ext. 2168 or ext. 2169
Web site: http://www.unitedskate.com

## World Cup Skateboarding

(530) 426-1502
e-mail: danielle@wcsk8.com
Web site: http://www.wcsk8.com

# Web Sites

Due to the changing nature of Internet links, the Rosen Publishing Group, Inc., has developed an online list of Web sites related to the subject of this book. This site is updated regularly. Please use this link to access the list:

http://www.rosenlinks.com/rs/sktt/

# For Further Reading

Bermudez, Ben. *Go Skate: The Monge's Guide to Skateboarding.* New York: 17th Street Press, 2001.

Brooke, Michael. *The Concrete Wave: The History of Skateboarding*. Toronto: Warwick Publishing, 1999.

Brooke, Michael. *SK8 Legends*. Milford, CT: Olmstead Press, 2001.

Jackson, Jay. *Skateboarding Basics*. Mankato, MN: Capstone Press, 1996.

Powell, Ben, et. al. *Skateboarding*. New York: Barron's Juveniles, 1999.

Rosenberg, Aaron. *A Beginner's Guide to Very Cool Skateboarding Tricks*. New York: The Rosen Publishing Group, Inc., 2003.

Werner, Doug, and Steve Badillo. *Skateboarder's Start-Up: A Beginner's Guide to Skateboarding*. Chula Vista, CA: Tracks Publishing, 2000.

# Bibliography

Brooke, Michael. *The Concrete Wave: The History of Skateboarding.* Toronto: Warwick Publishing, 1999.

Doherty, Paul, et. al. "Skateboard Science." Retrieved March 14, 2002 (http://www.exploratorium.edu/skateboarding).

Gould, Marilyn. *Skateboarding.* Mankato, MN: Capstone Press, 1991.

"How to Skateboard." Retrieved March 14, 2002 (http://www.geocities.com/jamen333).

Jackson, Jay. *Skateboarding Basics.* Mankato, MN: Capstone Press, 1996.

Shoemaker, Joel. *Skateboarding Streetstyle.* Mankato, MN: Capstone Press, 1995.

"Skateboard.com: Skate 101." Retrieved March 14, 2002 (http://www.skateboard.com/frontside/101).

Thatcher, Kevin J., and Brian Bannon. *Thrasher: The Radical Skateboard Book.* New York: Random House, 1992.

Utter, Jeff. "Beginner's Skateboarding Tutorial." Retrieved March 14, 2002 (http://www.smithandfeeble.com/b_tutorial/tutcontents.html).

# Index

## About the Author

Edward Willett is the author of more than twenty books, including young adult science fiction and fantasy novels, computer books, and nonfiction children's books on topics ranging from Ebola to careers in outer space. He also writes a weekly science column for newspapers and radio, hosts a TV show about computers, and is a professional actor and singer.

Ed lives in Regina, Saskatchewan, Canada, with his wife, Margaret Anne, and daughter, Alice. You can visit Ed online at www.edwardwillett.com.

## Acknowledgments

Thanks to Sean Barley

## Credits

Cover © Duomo/Corbis; pp. 4–5 © Richard Hamilton Smith/Corbis; p. 7 Hulton/Archive/Getty Images; pp. 11, 12, 14, 17–21, 24–33, 35, 36, 38 © Tony Donaldson/Icon SMI.

## Editor

Mark Beyer

## Design and Layout

Les Kanturek

BRENTWOOD PUBLIC LIBRARY
8765 Eulalie Ave.
Brentwood, MO 63144